Jordin
Tootoo

Jordin Tootoo

The highs and lows in the journey of the first Inuk player in the NHL

Melanie Florence

James Lorimer & Company, Ltd., Publishers
Toronto

James Lorimer & Company Ltd., Publishers acknowledges the support of the
Ontario Arts Council. We acknowledge the financial support of the Government
of Canada through the Canada Book Fund for our publishing activities. We
acknowledge the support of the Canada Council for the Arts for our publishing
program. We acknowledge the Government of Ontario through the Ontario
Media Development Corporation's Ontario Book Initiative.

The Canada Council | Le Conseil des Arts
for the Arts | du Canada

ONTARIO ARTS COUNCIL
CONSEIL DES ARTS DE L'ONTARIO

Cover design: Meredith Bangay

Library and Archives Canada Cataloguing in Publication
Florence, Melanie
      Jordin Tootoo : the highs and lows in the journey of the first Inuit
to play in the NHL / Melanie Florence.

(Record books)
Issued also in an electronic format.
ISBN 978-1-55277-531-8 (bound).—ISBN 978-1-55277-529-5 (pbk.)

      1. Tootoo, Jordin, 1983- —Juvenile literature. 2. Inuit hockey
players—Biography—Juvenile literature. I. Title. II. Series: Record books

CURR GV848.5.T66F56 2010   j796.962092   C2010-904070-8

James Lorimer & Company Ltd., Publishers
317 Adelaide Street West,
Suite #1002
Toronto, ON, Canada
M5V 1P9
www.lorimer.ca

Distributed in the United
States by:
Orca Book Publishers
P.O. Box 468
Custer, WA USA
98240-0468

Printed and bound in Canada.

MIX
Paper from
responsible sources
FSC® C004071

For Josh and Taylor, who inspire me and for all the children who aspire to follow their dreams just like Jordin did.

Contents

Prologue

It's cold in the arena. But for a guy who plays in a rink that's about minus twenty back home, this is nothing.

The sound of blades cutting a path across the ice can be heard above the screams of the fans. The sound of the player's own breathing rasps in his ears. He leans to the left and turns easily. He sees the puck out of the corner of his eye. He glides over to it. In one smooth, fluid motion, he lifts his stick high into the air. He pauses for a split second before bringing it down. A satisfying crack sounds off the ice. The puck soars across the ice to a teammate, who moves it toward the net.

He sees another player skating toward his teammate, intent on stealing the puck. Ice sprays as he skids to a stop, then takes off again. Gaining power as he gets closer and closer, he's at top speed by the time he reaches the other side of the rink. He passes players without looking. Without slowing, he hones in on his target. He angles his head down and clocks the other player with his shoulder. Hard. They both go down. The crowd goes wild. His reputation as a player is built on hits like this. Playing all out and hitting hard is how he played back home with his older brother. It's who he is. He sees no reason to change now. The fans are on their feet screaming and chanting, "Tootoo! Tootoo! Tootoo!" Before he can even notice the sound of his name echoing through the building,

Jordin Tootoo is off down the ice, already focusing on the next hit, the next play, the next goal.

1 From the Frozen North

Just below the Arctic Circle is a small Inuit community called Rankin Inlet. It lies on the western shore of Hudson Bay. With a population of just over 2,000 people, Rankin Inlet is one of the largest towns in Nunavut, Canada's biggest and newest territory. This is where the NHL's Jordin Tootoo calls home.

For 5,000 years the Inuit people have lived in the Far North. Their lifestyle has changed over the years, but some traditional ways remain. For them, home is a place where hunting caribou and whales, and fishing for arctic char take the place of shopping at local grocery stores.

At one time, the Inuit lived in temporary snow homes called igloos. Now they live in permanent wooden homes brought up from the south, where trees can grow. It was in an igloo in 1918 that Jordin Tootoo's grandmother, Jenny Tootoo, was born. Jenny was raised "on the

---

"Nooh-na-voot"

Nunavut was formed on April 1, 1999. It gave the Inuit control over their own government. Its name means "our land" in Inuktitut, the Inuit language. Its motto is "Nunavut, our strength." Nunavut covers around two million square kilometres (800,000 square miles) but has a population of only about 28,000. This makes it one of the least densely populated places on Earth.

---

land." With no gas or electricity for heat, and no supermarkets from which to buy food, Jenny learned to live as her ancestors had, by hunting the animals and fish the Arctic provided. Jenny raised her thirteen children to be survivors and to respect the land and what it had to offer them.

Using a traditional fishing rod, a young Jordin enjoys ice fishing at home near Rankin Inlet.

Jenny's son Barney Tootoo was born in Churchill, Manitoba. He was taught the traditional ways to provide for his family, just as his father was before him. Barney met and married Rose, a Canadian girl of Ukrainian descent.

Barney made his living as a miner. Later he became a plumber. He moved his family Rankin Inlet. Here, he and Rose would raise their two sons, Terence and Jordin, and their daughter, Corinne. Barney expected his boys to be survivors. He showed them how to hunt and fish, and taught them about the culture of their people.

Before most kids were old enough to have sleepovers, brothers Terence and Jordin were camping out by themselves. They were hunting game as big as beluga whales to bring home to their mother's table. Once, a blizzard caught Barney, Terence, and Jordin by surprise during a

Jordin, Terence, and Barney bundled up against the cold.

fishing trip. They were stranded out on the ice for four days. Barney stayed calm. He expected seven-year-old Jordin and ten-year-old Terence to do the same. The boys lived up to his hopes.

When they did kill an animal, it was shared among family and friends. For many generations the Inuit have relied on each other's generosity to survive. This was true when Jordin was growing up in the 1980s and 1990s, and it is still true today. If someone in the family or community needs something, they are taken care of. In Rankin Inlet, everyone is either family or friend. Doors are left unlocked and people come and go freely between each other's homes.

Jordin's mother, Rose, was the backbone of the Tootoo clan. But she was strict. This tended to scare other kids away when they visited Jordin and Terence. "They used to complain that they didn't have any friends because they were all afraid of me," Rose says with a laugh.

But Rose loved her family more than anything in the world. Her husband agrees. "She roars like a lion but is a kitty inside," he says. Widely known in the community, Rose was a good friend, a loving wife, and, to her three children, the best mother in the world.

"You know with my mom, she's one of those kind of ladies that are in your face," says Jordin with a laugh. "That's probably

The Tootoo children show off after a successful hunt.

where I get most of my toughness, from my mother. She likes the roughness."

Everyone has to be tough in Rankin Inlet. It is a place so remote that it can't be reached by car. A couple of times a year a barge comes by to bring supplies. But even staple foods are hard to come by and the prices make it nearly impossible to survive on store-bought items alone. So children learn to hunt at a very young age. They can handle quads, boats, and rifles with ease. Jordin shot his first wolf at the age of twelve.

Terence and Jordin: best friends.

Some non-Inuit people have argued that the Inuit shouldn't have special rights to hunt and harvest Arctic animals. But with store-bought food so expensive, hunting and fishing are still the most common and easiest way to get food to eat.

Many of Rankin Inlet's inhabitants will never leave their home. They will visit with friends, they will go to work, they will access the outside world through the Internet. They will travel around the town's rocky terrain on four-wheelers called quads, past hotels, cafes, and restaurants. But there are still some modern conveniences missing — like fast food. "For us, fast food is when you shoot an animal and eat it right there," Jordin jokes.

Jordin Tootoo was four when he laced up

Jordin as a boy relaxing at home with his video games.

2 Hockey — Tootoo Style

his first pair of skates. Jordin and his brother, Terence, grew up watching their dad play hockey. Barney had made a name for himself as right wing in the Northern Manitoba Senior Leagues. He was a tough player, but smaller than a lot of the others. Quick with the puck, he wasn't afraid to hit bigger players. He played with heart and determination. These qualities he would pass on to his sons.

Origins of the Game

There is a lot of debate about the origins of hockey in Canada. Some people claim it was first played in Windsor, Ontario. Others say it was first played by British soldiers stationed in the Maritimes. The Mi'kmaq, an aboriginal group from eastern Canada, played a similar game before Europeans arrived. The Mi'kmaq played on skates made from sharpened animal bones. They used a frozen apple as a puck. Wooden sticks were carved from hornbeam trees.

Barney's boys learned to play hockey on any frozen surface they could find. There is little traffic in Rankin Inlet, so street hockey meant skating up and down the town's frozen roads. Players skated hard enough to sweat in the minus fifty degree temperatures.

In 1985, the community built an arena inside a steel-shelled building. Before that, Rankin Inlet's first rink was a tiny building

Rankin Inlet, where Jordin grew up, is a remote community just below the Arctic Circle.

called The Dome. The Dome was lit with one streetlight and the ice was made with spaghetti to keep it from cracking. Its biggest advantage was keeping the skaters sheltered from the wind. Players had to make some of their own equipment. The goalie wore a piece of plywood tied to a sealskin mitten to block, and a padded mitten to catch the puck. The Dome was a fire hazard and it closed a few years later.

The new rink that Jordin played in was

still unlike indoor rinks in the south. There was no cooling system in the building. The ice was natural, and the temperature in the rink was kept at around minus twenty to keep the ice surface frozen. The surface usually didn't freeze until November and melted by mid-April.

Barney was the arena manager. As a

Jordin (bottom row, second from left) with his team in Rankin Inlet.

former player it was only natural for him to coach his sons. In 1989-90, the Rankin Inlet Minor Hockey Association formed. It was a house league that played three times a week. Every other day, the boys could be found using any bit of ice for pickup games.

Barney expected hockey to be played rough. His sons were to be as tough on the ice as they were on the land. He had little sympathy for them when they fell or got frustrated on the ice.

With only enough kids for one team per age group, they all played each other and made up the rules as they went. The isolation and lack of money made it impossible to fly to other communities for regular games. The kids from Rankin Inlet scrimmaged and played pickup games on the frozen water of Williamson Lake. They would save up to go to one tournament a year.

Terence was a hard hitter from the start.

Avataq Cup

The Avataq Cup is played yearly in Rankin Inlet. It is the biggest hockey tournament in the territory. Teams from all over Nunavut, including Coral Harbour, Repulse Bay, Baker Lake, and the capital, Iqaluit, fly in for the event. The tournament is named after a ship that sank in Hudson Bay in 2000 while carrying supplies to the northern communities.

With a three-year age gap between brothers, Jordin was usually at the receiving end of those hits. Barney told his younger son that he could play with the older kids only when he could fight his way through them.

Jordin recalls, "My brother and his friends were always hard on me. That's where I got my toughness. They'd tell me to body check the boards at full speed, and I'd do it. They just wanted to laugh at me, but when you're nine and they're twelve, it's intimidating. My dad always told me, 'If you want to play with the older kids, you'll have to stick up for yourself.' He'd just laugh when I got beat up by my brother and his friends."

This treatment by his brother and older teammates may have seemed harsh, but it paid off. The older Jordin got, the more dangerous he became on the ice. He was really living up to his Inuit name, Kudluk,

Jordin (bottom row, third from left) and his teammates. Barney is the coach.

the word for "thunder."

The brothers practised long into the summer nights, shooting slapshots into plywood boards. In the house, they ruined the rec room walls by shooting at them in the winter. By the time he hit his teens, Jordin had a terrifying slapshot. Goalies would leave the net empty when they saw him coming rather than face getting hit by a lightning-fast puck.

The Tootoo brothers were like a force of nature. They played fearlessly and tirelessly through the cold, the snow, and the long endless nights. They cut down their opponents in yearly tournaments. Their first, when Jordin was twelve or thirteen, was an eye-opener for them. They didn't know that there were actual rules to follow in the game. Jordin fought his opponents the same way he fought his friends. As a result, he ended up being suspended from the game. But the underdogs from Rankin Inlet dominated. And the other teams feared them.

3 Leaving Home

The Tootoo brothers got as good as they were going to get playing hockey at home in Rankin Inlet. Barney knew that they had dreams of playing in the National Hockey League. As their coach, he realized they would have to leave home to do it.

"We knew if they wanted to further their careers and lives they'd have to leave. It was difficult. Really difficult," said Rose. "We have very close, tight-knit families and they just can't bear the thought of letting their children go. Many [kids] have tried and many have come back."

For the Tootoos, home was a place where they were almost as likely to find a polar bear on their doorstep as a friend. They were more likely to see a canoe than a car. Things would be different for the brothers away from home, more different than they ever imagined.

They could barely afford it, but the Tootoo family was willing to make sacrifices to see the boys succeed. "Let them see what's out there," Barney told people.

The chance came for Jordin when a junior team spotted him playing in an Aboriginal tournament as a member of the Young Bulls peewee team in Fort Providence, Northwest Territories. They were impressed. They offered him a spot on the Spruce Grove Broncos in Alberta. So, at fourteen, Jordin was given a one-

Jordin working his way up the ranks.

way ticket to play in the AAA Bantam league. Terence, now seventeen, left for Manitoba to play Junior A hockey.

What a change Spruce Grove was from Rankin Inlet! The sights and sounds of traffic overwhelmed Jordin. All those cars speeding past! He'd never seen a stoplight before. He'd never seen an ATM. He'd never eaten at a McDonald's or a Taco

Bell. He hadn't even see trees growing back home. "A lot of times I just stayed inside," he said. After the quiet of Rankin Inlet, the noise and fast pace of the city was a huge shock.

Jordin was placed with a billet family, the Pesonys. They gave him a place to live, and were as close to family as he had while he was away from home.

"I had never been away from my family, so I was pretty nervous about everything. It was culture shock for me, but my billet

Home Away from Home

A billet family in the junior hockey league provides a home for players from out of province or country. The family commits to a full school year of care. They invite the player completely into their home and make them part of the family. They support the athlete by attending games and helping them get used to a new city.

Jordin and his trophies.

family played a big role in helping me to adjust to everything. It was helpful that my billet family was Native, but I received lots of support from my mom and dad as well."

But as good as his billet family was to

him, it didn't make up for the fact that Jordin was separated from his brother. "We're pretty close, you know. Some other brothers in other families . . . they're just not like me and Terence. We stick up for each other. We're there for each other and we know we've got each other's back. Terence is my best friend. Always will be."

Back home, Jordin and Terence had done everything together. Where you saw one, you saw the other. So it was hard for Jordin to be away from home and from Terence.

Jordin got phone calls from home and care packages of beluga whale and caribou from his mother. This helped ease his homesickness a little. But he knew what he had to do. "At some point you have to be able to adjust to life in the outside world. I was nervous, but all I focused on was playing hockey. I knew that if I wanted to make it playing hockey, I would have to get comfortable living away from my family and friends for awhile."

After leaving Rankin Inlet, Jordin encountered racism for the first time. Where he grew up, nearly everyone looked alike and celebrated the same culture. The only thing that had set Jordin apart from other kids was his skill on the ice.

"I was the only Inuk in the area [Spruce Grove], and for the first time I experienced racism at school. I was living with a friend, Justin Pesony, who was Aboriginal, and gangs of kids would come to the house yelling that we weren't going to take over their school," Jordin remembers.

To the local kids, there was no difference between the Inuk and his Aboriginal friend. They were both targets of abuse because of the way they looked. Jordin tried to avoid trouble, but the neighbourhood kids loved to torment him. One day, Jordin was walking home from school, and a gang of boys followed him. They taunted him and tried to get a reaction. One boy, egged on by his friends, reached out and knocked the schoolbooks out of Jordin's hands. The others quickly jumped in, pushing Jordin aside and laughing. One boy picked up a book, pulled out a lighter, and set Jordin's book on fire. Then he threw it down on the others.

As Jordin watched, they laughed and called him a "dumb Indian." He heard his father's words in his head. "Fight your way through," Barney had told his son before he left home. It was how Jordin had been raised. He didn't know any other way. Jordin figured that it had always worked for him before. "I had my battles off the ice. Little did they know I'm a crazy Inuk who eats raw meat and could butcher them up, no sweat," he jokes. "Eating that raw meat makes me a little wacko sometimes."

There were four of them, but Jordin never worried about the odds against him. He sized up the boys. Each one of them was

Indigenous Canadians

According to the federal government, the indigenous people of Canada are divided into three main groups: Inuit, Métis, and First Nations people. Inuit refers to the Aboriginal people of the Canadian Arctic. Métis refers to people of mixed European and Aboriginal descent. First Nations refers to those indigenous people who don't fit into the other two categories.

larger and meaner-looking than he was.

Jordin threw only four punches that day. He didn't need any more than that.

"I took that negative situation and turned it into something to motivate me in a positive direction. I couldn't let it get to my head. I think that is where many young Native players get discouraged. I know people were jealous and wanted me to fail, but that only made me try harder to succeed," Jordin explained.

He brought that same attitude to the ice. During his first home game in Spruce Grove, Jordin got into a brawl with another player. Jordin beat him so badly that he got a seven-game suspension. Jordin was confused. He didn't understand why he was being punished. As far as he knew, anything goes on the ice. What was all the fuss about?

"The other teams thought we were crazy," he said. "We just played the same way we did [at home]. We didn't know any better. We didn't even know you got kicked out for fighting."

Jordin had never played with kids his own age before. He couldn't figure out why people kept telling him to back off and stop being so rough. But it was that edge, that fearlessness, that was going to help Jordin succeed in his career.

4 Moving Up

Jordin played a whole season in the AAA Bantam League in Alberta. In the fall of 1998 he was ready to join Terence on the Opaskwayak Cree Nation Blizzard out of Manitoba. The OCN Blizzard was a Native Canadian Junior Team. The brothers thrived on the team. There were still some moments of culture shock and racism. But Jordin had his brother beside him. He felt stronger than ever.

The Tootoo brothers were physically

small by hockey standards, but they played big. Jordin and Terence were fearless on the ice. "My brother and I always looked after each other," Jordin said. "If he fought, I fought. We were wild."

"Playing with the OCN Blizzard was a great experience for me, especially since I got to play with my brother," Jordin remembers. Jordin was awarded Rookie of the Year, Most Popular Player, and Scholastic Player of the Year honours with the OCN Blizzard in the 1998–99 season.

The brothers also played together on Team Indigenous and competed in Finland. Their star was rising and they were making a name for themselves. They were living by their family motto: Not the best, but hard to beat.

Jordin and Terence looked alike. They played with the same style. But soon it became clear to everyone that Jordin was developing his hockey skills and growing as a player faster than his brother.

Team Indigenous

Team Indigenous began in 1999 when former NHL player and coach Ted Nolan suggested to Grand Chief Phil Fontaine that they create a team of talented Aboriginal players. Expecting it to be a long process, Nolan was surprised when the Canadian Hockey League offered him a spot in a tournament in Finland just a month after Nolan and Fontaine met. They needed money fast, but the large Canadian corporations weren't interested in helping. The Aboriginal community stepped up and donated what they could. Lakehead University in Thunder Bay offered their campus for the team to train. That team included the Tootoo brothers. They travelled to Finland and competed in the Universal Players Hockey Tournament, an under-20 tournament that featured teams from Russia, the US, Sweden, and the host nation. Team Indigenous finished fifth.

In 1999, Jordin was drafted by the Brandon Wheat Kings in Manitoba. The

Wheat Kings were a Western Hockey League team. With the Wheat Kings, Jordin's reputation as a tough competitor grew. So did his skill.

On the ice, Jordin was a force to be reckoned with. He hit hard and played harder. He took 218.5 penalty minutes in four seasons. Twice he was suspended. He was rough and played just like he had back in Rankin Inlet.

Only 175 centimetres (5 feet 9 inches) tall and weighing 84 kilograms (185 pounds), he was shorter than most of the other players. But you would never know it by watching him play. Jordin played like he was a giant. He was a brawler who hit at full speed and showed no mercy. The crowd went wild when Jordin took to the ice. They were rarely disappointed.

Jordin Tootoo was voted the most popular player four years in a row with the Wheat Kings. He was also named best body checker and had the hardest slapshot, at an astounding 154.6 kilometres per hour (96.1 miles per hour). He was made captain of the Canadian Under 18 National Team for the 4-Nations tournament in Slovakia in 2000. There, he led his team to a gold-medal win.

Jordin and Terence were both trying to succeed in the same game. Some people might guess they were rivals. Some families in this situation might be in danger of being torn apart. But there was

Men's Under 18 Team

The Under 18 National Team is chosen each year to give promising athletes their first taste of international hockey. Each August, Hockey Canada holds a training camp for the best players across the country. At the end of camp, twenty-two players are chosen. Two-thirds of these players go on to play for the National Junior Team.

no jealousy between the Tootoo brothers. Terence was tough on Jordin when they were kids on the ice, but they grew up to be each other's biggest fans.

Between hockey seasons, the Tootoo brothers spent summers either at home or in Brandon. They trained and worked together. They sold Team Tootoo jerseys and caribou jerky on their website. To escape the sizzling summer heat in Manitoba, they'd hang out in a walk-in freezer to get a little feel of home.

On the road and back home in the North, Jordin and Terence visited schools and community centres to talk to kids. When someone approached them for an autograph, even if they were busy, Jordin and Terence took the time to make them feel special, especially their younger fans. The Tootoo brothers were always happy to take pictures, sign a photo, and chat with the young hockey fans.

Barney and Rose show off their Team Tootoo T-shirts.

The Tootoos were focused on their shared dream of playing in the NHL. They were Team Tootoo, and it seemed that nothing could stop their star from rising and their dreams from coming true.

In 2001, Terence Tootoo graduated from the OCN Blizzard. He went to the United

States to try out for the Roanoke Express. The Roanoke Express was a team only two ranks below the NHL in the East Coast Hockey League. Coming off a three-championship junior career with the OCN Blizzard, Terence was more than ready. He dazzled them at the tryouts. When he was offered a contract, history was made. Terence Tootoo became the first Inuk ever to play professional hockey. There was no one prouder of Terence than Jordin.

Then, on May 29, 2001, Jordin Tootoo made history when he became the first person of Inuit descent to be drafted by the NHL. He was 98th overall. Signing a three-year contract with the Nashville Predators was a dream come true for the eighteen-year-old from Rankin Inlet. It was made even more special by the fact that he got the call while on a speaking tour in Nunavut.

"It couldn't have happened in a better place," said Jordin. "I'm in the capital of

Big Leagues

The NHL is the "big show" of pro hockey. But there are other pro leagues for players. The American Hockey League (AHL) is one step below the NHL, and each AHL team is connected with an NHL team. Often players drafted to the NHL will spend time playing for an AHL "farm team," honing their skills and waiting for their chance to play on the NHL team. The East Coast Hockey League (ECHL) is a step down from the AHL. Promising young players start here, hoping to work their way up to the top.

Nunavut; I'm a Nunavut-born player. It's an honour to be the first. At the same time I know there are lots of talented kids up here who, if they put their mind to it, can attain their goals. I'm trying to pave the way for Aboriginal youth."

5 Tragedy Strikes

By the summer of 2002, it looked like nothing could stop the Tootoo brothers. Terence was looking forward to a second season with the Roanoke Express. He was eagerly getting ready for a tryout with the Norfolk Admirals. The Admirals were an AHL team only one step from the NHL. Jordin was looking forward to his NHL tryout with the Nashville Predators. He headed back to Brandon, Manitoba, for the Wheat Kings training camp.

Jordin was staying with Neil and Janene Roy. They had been his billet family the year before, too. Terence was in The Pas, Manitoba. He was waiting for the papers that would allow him to play in the United States. On August 27, Terence made the seven-hour drive to Brandon to spend a few days with his brother.

On August 28, Terence and Jordin joined friends for a night out. They were all laughing, talking, and having a great time. There was a lot of food and the drinks were flowing. They stayed out late that night.

Jordin decided to stay with a friend instead of going home. He tried to talk Terence into staying with him. But Terence wanted to get back to the Roys' house and go to bed. They said goodnight, and Jordin watched Terence drive off in his red SUV.

The next morning, the Roy family got up and found Terence's jacket and shoes. They assumed that he had come home the night before and was still asleep. The Roys ate breakfast, read the paper, and left for work. Minutes later, Neil Roy found a message on his voice mail. A police constable had called the night before. He left a message saying that Terence needed to speak to the Roys. Concerned, the Roys phoned the station. They were told that the arresting officer was off duty. "I don't think it's anything serious," they said. "There's no cause for alarm."

Jordin, meanwhile, had woken up at his friend's house that morning shrugging off the effects of his late night out. When Terence didn't show up for a workout they had planned, he began to worry. It wasn't like his brother to let him down, or to miss a chance to hang out with him. Jordin went to the Roys' house, looking for his brother. Other than the shoes and jacket Terence had worn the night before, there was no sign of him.

Where was Terence?

The morning passed achingly slow. Jordin felt that something was very wrong. He called his mother, who caught the next plane to Brandon.

By this time, the police were told of Terence's disappearance. Police dogs were brought in to help with the search for him. Jordin and Neil Roy waited nervously for word. They didn't have to wait long.

At 1:00 p.m., just ten minutes into the search, the dogs found the lifeless body of Terence Tootoo in the woods behind the Roys' house. There was a 12-gauge shotgun by his side. Terence had shot himself in the head. He was twenty-two years old.

Jordin was devastated. Terence, the person he loved most in the world, had left him a note. "Do well Jor. Go all the way. Take care of the family. You are the man. Ter."

Even in his worst moment, Terence was thinking of the brother he adored.

Details of what had happened after the

brothers had said goodnight came as a huge shock to Jordin. At about 3:00 a.m., Terence had been pulled over by the Brandon City Police on suspicion of drunk driving. The police arrested Terence, impounded his vehicle, and took him to the station. There, Terence was charged with impaired driving. He blew 0.19 on a Breathalyzer (the legal limit is 0.08). He was released on a notice to appear for a court date. The police then dropped him off at the Roys'.

It was there that the police made a fatal mistake. Brandon police procedure states that anyone charged with a DUI must be placed in the care of a sober adult. But the police didn't wake up the Roys. Terence was dropped off and left at the front door alone.

No one knows for certain what went through Terence's mind that night. What is known is that Terence was well aware of being a role model back home and would not have wanted to let anyone down. He probably realized that he had done something that might affect his ability to play in the United States. Even worse, he could have seen his NHL dreams vanishing. With a heavy heart, and still under the influence of the alcohol he had at dinner, Terence would have taken off his shoes and gone to bed.

The Roys believe that Terence waited until the next morning after they had left for work. When there was no one else home, Terence got one of Neil's rifles from the shed. He walked into the woods behind the house, and ended his own life.

While Jordin was dealing with the terrible shock of Terence's death, Rose Tootoo landed in Brandon. She still believed that her elder son was only missing. It was when she arrived in Brandon that she was told that Terence had been found dead.

The news spread quickly. Everyone who knew Terence reacted with shock. His

After Terence's death, the Roanoke Express retired the number 22 in his honour. No Roanoke player would ever wear Terence Tootoo's number again.

grieving family was left wondering if there was something they could have done. "I think he thought [the DUI] was the end of his life," his mother told a reporter at the time, "that his hockey career was going down the drain."

"Knowing Terence and how proud he was of his heritage, and knowing how proud people in his town and our town were of him, maybe he felt he let them down," Terence's coach, Perry Florio said. "But that was not the case. People make mistakes all the time."

Whether they knew him personally or simply as a well-loved player for the Roanoke Express, people loved and missed Terence Tootoo.

A nameless fan posted a message online at the Hockeytown Centre bulletin board: "Here in Virginia we feel we have lost a son. He would come out every night after a game and talk with us and sign for the kids. We are just so blessed to have gotten to know him and love him even if for a short time. He was only in Virginia for one season but his personality and kindness has had an impact on everyone who met him or watched him play."

The Tootoo family, Rankin Inlet, and Terence's teammates mourned the loss of a brother, a son, a hometown boy, and a talented athlete. Terence had felt the pressure of being a role model and of his vow to never let anyone down. That pressure was now on Jordin.

Tragic Stats

Suicide among Inuit men is one of the biggest social problems in the Far North. Compared to men between the ages of fifteen and twenty-four in southern Canada, Inuit men are twenty-eight times more likely to kill themselves. Many factors are to blame. Some people blame the long, dark arctic winters, problems with alcohol and drug addiction, and dealing with relationship problems or abuse.

6 Playing Through the Pain

With the grief of losing his brother and best friend weighing heavily on him, Jordin did the only thing he could think of to do. He played hockey.

The day after Terence's suicide, Jordin surprised everyone by asking to be taken to the rink. He sat silently watching the Wheat Kings' tryouts.

The Nashville Predators offered to let Jordin skip tryouts to be with his family. But Jordin knew that the one place he could be closest to Terence was on the ice, with a hockey stick in his hand.

Jordin left for Nashville, Tennessee. He was ready to take on a new challenge and ready to clear his head. Early September is blisteringly hot in Nashville. For a guy from Nunavut, it was nearly unbearable. Jordin ran between air-conditioned buildings. He played his heart out at tryouts. He worked harder than he ever had in his life. But he didn't quite make it.

Jordin went back to Brandon. He changed his number to 22. It had been Terence's number, a play on their name — Tootoo. Jordin stencilled Terence's name on all of his hockey sticks. Then he threw himself into what would be his last season with the Wheat Kings. He earned five points in his first game, and 57 in the next 34. "[Terence] was the guy I lived and died for," said Jordin. "If it wasn't for him being by my side, I don't think I'd be this strong person."

December came. Canada chose Jordin for the World Juniors team. He travelled with them to Halifax, Nova Scotia. There, he dominated the ice. He played the way he and Terence had grown up playing. Jordin was named Canada's Player of the Game when they beat the Czech Republic 4–0 to win the silver medal. His family was in the stands, cheering him on.

While Jordin could enjoy his successes on the ice, off the ice he had time to think. That was the hardest for him. He told a reporter who asked about Terence that he just wanted to play hockey and not think of anything else. But at night and on the bus, he had hours to himself. All he could do was wonder why his brother didn't call him that night in August.

But every time he stepped onto the ice, he felt his brother right there with him. "It's almost like there's two of us playing in one body now," he said.

The year 2002 was the saddest and most difficult of Jordin's life. But it had its good points too. Aside from his achievements on the ice, Jordin was honoured with a National Aboriginal Achievement Award. It was also the year that Nunavut Premier Paul Okalik named Jordin as an "official role model" for the Government of Nunavut's poster campaign. Jordin appeared on posters designed to inspire kids to stay in school and to set goals for themselves. There was no better subject than an Inuk who made it all the way to the National Hockey League.

An Aboriginal Honour

The National Aboriginal Achievement Awards represent one of the highest honours that can be awarded to successful people in Native communities. The recipients are considered role models. The awards show, which is broadcast nationally, is a platform to show Aboriginal youth what they can achieve with hard work and perseverance.

7 A Born Predator

Jordin had been drafted by the Nashville Predators in 2001. It was finally time for him to do what he had been training for and dreaming about since he was a kid back in Rankin Inlet.

October 9, 2003, Jordin Tootoo made history as the first Inuk to play in the National Hockey League.

At least forty of his family and friends travelled by plane, bus, and car from Rankin Inlet. They came to Nashville to support

Jordin Tootoo playing for the Nashville Predators.

Jordin and the Predators as they got ready to play the Mighty Ducks of Anaheim.

Rose and Barney, decked out in their Team Tootoo jerseys, sat a few rows behind the Predators bench. With them was Jordin and Terence's sister, Corinne. They waited nervously with Rankin Inlet's Mayor, Lorne Kusugak. Nunavut Premier Paul Okalik took vacation time to be there.

CBC News spoke to the Premier, who proudly said, "It's a story for all Inuit in Canada because he's the first Inuk to ever play and that is quite something, a very special thing that I never thought I'd see in my own lifetime."

Jordin's cousin Victor was there. He was ready to cheer on Jordin with the Nunavut flag painted on his face. He told the same reporter, "Every television set in Rankin Inlet is tuned to this game." And he was right. The streets back home were empty. Everyone gathered together in front of their TVs to watch their hometown hero make history.

Jordin was more than ready for his NHL debut. But one important thing was missing — Terence. Jordin felt Terence's presence and dedicated his game to him. He had the number 22 inside a heart drawn on the back of his skates. He had a framed picture of his brother in his locker. When he went on the ice, Terence was there in spirit.

"I know he's up there looking down on me, giving me a high-five. This is what he'd love to become one day, a pro player," Jordin said. The brothers had shared the same dream. They wanted to step onto the ice as the first Inuit player in the NHL with family and friends in the stands.

Finally realizing a lifelong dream after years of hard work was something that would take a few days to sink in. At this moment, Jordin's head was already in the game. He was determined to play his game, just like he had for every other team he had ever played for.

Only 59 seconds into the first period, Jordin Tootoo, the right wing from Nunavut, took to the ice for the first time as an NHL player. He had spent most of his life preparing for that moment, but Jordin was still nervous. He heard his name announced over the loudspeaker. He knew that his parents had heard it too. Jordin had one thought running through his head. "I just didn't want to trip over the boards coming out," he said.

A nervous Tootoo was feeling the pressure. Nashville coach Barry Trotz made the decision to take him out for a few shifts to give him time to calm down. The strategy worked. In the third period, a more composed Jordin did what he did best. He went out and drew a penalty. Forty-two seconds later, the Predators scored the game-winning goal.

The Predators celebrated a 3–1 victory over the Mighty Ducks of Anaheim. Jordin's family couldn't have been more proud of their son if he had made the winning goal himself.

"It's finally sunk in now that he's playing, the pressure is off his wide shoulders," his father beamed at ESPN reporters. "He seems to be holding his own out there. He looks pretty good."

Rose agreed. "It's awesome, I think I would have liked to see him have a little scrap," she laughed. Like Jordin, she felt Terence's presence at that first game. "We know Jordin's brother would have loved to be there too," she said.

Already a household name in Nunavut, Jordin Tootoo went on to impress hockey fans across Canada and in Nashville. They respected the hard-hitting right wing, and his popularity grew. Surprised at his short stature, some American hockey fans

Jordin backed against the boards with the puck.

laughed when they saw him take to the ice. But they didn't laugh for long. Jordin never forgot the lessons he had learned from his father and brother on the cold lakes of Rankin Inlet. He saw no reason to change the way he played just because he had finally made it to "the show."

Another big night in Jordin's young career came on Thursday, October 16, 2003, when the Nashville Predators played the St. Louis Blues.

The score was all tied up at 1–1. The

action had fans on the edge of their seats. Players zigzagged across the ice, trying to get the puck, passing it to their teammates and stealing it from their opponents. Jordin was weaving between players, keeping a close eye on the puck. He was watching for his chance.

And there it was. The perfect opportunity. Jordin took it. He grabbed the puck and smoothly fed it to Dan Hamhuis. Hamhuis made a stunning wrist shot that flew past Blues goalie Chris Osgood like a rocket. And just like that, amid the screams of Preds fans, Jordin Tootoo made an assist. He had earned his first point in the NHL.

That Thursday also marked the first time NHL fans would see Jordin in a fight. During the second period, Jordin and Mike Danton (#22 for the Blues) dropped their gloves, threw off their helmets, and traded blows. The result of that quick brawl? Five minutes in the

Tootoo Firsts

- 1st NHL goal: October 23, 2003 against the Atlanta Thrashers.
- 1st Gordie Howe Hat Trick (a goal, an assist, and a fighting major in one game): January 10, 2004 against the St. Louis Blues.
- 1st Playoff goal: April 10, 2008 against the Detroit Red Wings; Game 1 of the Western Conference Quarter Finals.

penalty box for each of them. The inside of the penalty box would become very familiar to Tootoo. The spitfire right wing would go on to become one of the top brawlers in the league.

In no time, Jordin gained a reputation for being fearless. He became what is known in hockey as an agitator. His role on the Preds was to rile up the other team. He was to irritate them so much that they would become distracted and make mistakes. It was a role he excelled in.

Unlike most agitators, Jordin didn't use insults or low blows to frustrate the opposing team. He used brute force. He punished them with big hits into the boards at full speed. For his unstoppable drive, he became known as the "Tootoo Train." His fans blew train whistles when he came on the ice. They leaped into standing ovations when he sent another player into the boards.

But what went through Jordin's mind when he took to the ice? Did he hear the screams and the chants? Did it affect his game? For Jordin, it was all about playing the game the way he played it growing up. His game.

"The more you think out there, the more nervous you get. I just do what I do best, skate well and use my linemates," he said. His linemates appreciated the powerhouse forward. The opposing teams didn't.

You might wonder what it's like to be

in a fight, to face down an opponent with no fear. What does Jordin Tootoo think when he throws off his gloves and gets ready to fight? What is running through his head as he circles a player who is bigger and heavier than he is? "Get a punch in," he laughs. "And don't get hit!"

But an agitator will get hit. How does a player prepare for that? How does a player not get distracted? "You can't play with fear," Jordin says. "If you fear getting hurt, that's when it happens. You have to play with confidence and with heart."

No one has a bigger heart than Jordin Tootoo. He must feel something when he hits someone so hard they're taken off the ice on a stretcher. When your opponent is bleeding on the ice, how do you keep playing the game? He says, "When you face adversity, you have to be able to zone things out. You control the play with the right mindset."

Jordin definitely has that mindset. Whether he plays against a friend, a rival, or someone he admires and respects, his game remains the same. It isn't anything personal. Jordin is as single-minded when he plays hockey as when he was out hunting back home. He has total concentration and an ability to shut out everything around him and just focus on the job at hand. And the other teams take notice.

When the fans blow their whistles and scream his name, Toots plays his heart out. When his jersey became the top-seller of the Preds players, he remained focused. He was persistent. Even if the other teams don't like him, they have to respect him.

"He definitely knows how to get the crowd going," said Erik Reitz, who played for the Minnesota Wild. "Some guys are big and tough, but they don't know how to agitate and push the other team's buttons. He's definitely someone you

Tootoo steals the puck.

don't like to play against."

And that was Jordin's job. He was drilling other players into the boards and frustrating the other teams. When he's on the ice, he doesn't let up — not for a second.

"There are some guys around the league known as tough guys or pests, but the real good ones are in your face every shift," said Barret Jackman, defense for the

Blues. "When you get hit once a period, you don't think about it too much. But when you get hit every shift by a guy like Jordin, you're aware."

Jordin doesn't stoop to rude or personal comments on the ice. But he knows how to annoy the other team. "When they do try to talk to me, I just zone them out and play between the whistles," he laughed. "I might give them a wink or a smile. That makes them even madder."

Another person who appreciates his persistence is Predators Head Coach Barry Trotz. "Everyone gives him their two cents from the bench," he said. "But they don't give him as much when he's on the ice . . . He'll have 15 guys yapping at him and then when they go on the ice, nobody's yapping at him."

It's Hockey in Any Language

On January 30, 2010, two CBC broadcasters called an NHL game in Inuktitut. Inuktitut is the most commonly spoken language in Nunavut. The game featured two Canadian teams, the Ottawa Senators and the Montreal Canadiens. Although Charlie Panigoniak and Annie Ford called the game in Inuktitut, broadcasting problems left many fans in Nunavik watching the game on mute and listening to the broadcast on their radios.

8 Fighting Through

Every agitator in the NHL is accused of dirty play and using too much force at some point. Jordin is no exception. To some he is a thug and to others a hero.

One of the most talked-about fights of Jordin's career was on March 17, 2007, in a game against the Dallas Stars. Late in the third period, Jordin made a clean hit on Stars centre Mike Modano. The hit sent both of them to the ice.

Stars defenseman Stephane Robidas

came skating in to defend his teammate. Jordin saw Robidas approach out of the corner of his eye. He turned and laid Robidas out on the ice with one punch to the face. Modano, who by that time was up on his feet, slashed Tootoo across the back with his stick. The referees broke it up before Jordin could retaliate.

All of this happened in a matter of seconds. It probably would have become just another hit on Jordin's already lengthy resumé, but Stephane Robidas was taken off the ice on a stretcher. He was unconscious and had a concussion.

As a result, Robidas was given a minor penalty for charging. Tootoo received a double-minor penalty for roughing, and was suspended for five games.

Hockey is a sport where fights are expected to break out. Many viewers look forward to them. In such a sport, who is at fault for a fight that results in an injury?

Comments by journalists, sports reporters, and fans were flying fast and furious. From fan forums to ESPN, everyone was talking about it.

Said one fan, "Tootoo made a nice hit on Modano, saw that Robidas was coming in gearing up to take his head off . . . So Tootoo, instead of LETTING Robidas take his head off, does something about it? If Tootoo did nothing, he could have been seriously injured . . . so he did what he thought he needed to do to protect himself."

Another posted: "Funny, I really don't see anything wrong with what Tootoo did on that play. I did, however, find Modano's little stick swing at the end of it to be a dirty move. Robidas knew exactly what he was going in for, a shot or two on Tootoo's beak and instead got drilled before he could get a few shots off himself. Watch the replay, his gloves are aimed right at Tootoo's head."

With a black eye, Jordin poses with a fan after a game.

But not all the fans supported Tootoo's innocence.

"You can't just start swinging at every head around you in a blind manner. That's what he did. Turn around. See who you're dancing with and man up, if that's the

NHL way. You don't put on your toe picks and start clocking anyone and everyone around you."

"Tootoo didn't have to punch the guy in the head . . . he could easily just put his hands up and pushed back if he wanted to defend himself. Big difference between getting your hands up and using a big right hook."

In addition to the fans' comments, the athletes and coaches made statements to the press.

"I take full responsibility for my actions and accept the consequences," said Tootoo. "I maintain my actions were taken in self-defence. I am sorry to see another player get injured and I wish Robidas well in his recovery."

Robidas himself said he was blindsided by the punch.

"There's different ways to see it, I guess. But what I remember is I went in and had

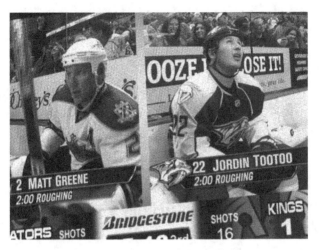

Jordin Tootoo is no stranger to the penalty box. He is one of the NHL's toughest players.

my stick down and my gloves on," Robidas told the Dallas Morning News. "If I go in and try to jump him, that's my fault. But I'm just going in there to let him know, 'Hey, you don't hit Modano like that, and if you want to go, we'll go.' That's all I was doing. I wasn't going to jump him, but then, boom."

Predators General Manager David

Poile added his thoughts. "Jordin was put in a very difficult situation with Robidas confronting him. I don't know what he was supposed to do. All he could see was a player coming at him with his arms up and certainly looking like he's ready to enter into some form of confrontation. I think Jordin did what I think everybody would do, and he reacted and threw a punch."

NHL senior executive vice-president and director of hockey operations Colin Campbell disagreed. "While a player is entitled to defend himself, Mr. Tootoo's forceful blow to Robidas' head was an overly aggressive and inappropriate response."

Predators coach Barry Trotz might have said it best: "If you feel like you are getting attacked you have to protect yourself. I would stand behind that. You can't tell me that Toots didn't feel like he was under attack. Robidas wasn't coming over there to give him a kiss."

Jordin took his suspension without complaint and the Predators decided not to challenge it. Five games later, Toots was back on the ice, making big hits and getting under the skin of the other teams.

Fight Night

The rules of hockey fighting are very specific. Both players must drop their sticks (so they can't be used as weapons) and immediately shake off their gloves to fight bare-knuckled. If a ref warns players to end the fight, they must immediately stop. If they don't, they face a game misconduct penalty and the possibility of fines or suspension. Some linesmen will allow a fight to continue until one or both players end up on the ice. Officials will break up a fight that looks one-sided, when a player gains too much of an advantage, when more than two players are involved, or when there have been multiple fights.

9 Life off the Ice

Being the first Inuk player in the National Hockey League has its perks. But it also comes with the pressures of fame.

Within Canada's Aboriginal communities, especially Inuit communities, there is no bigger hero than Jordin Tootoo. Kids, especially, look up to him and Jordin takes that responsibility very seriously. There is nothing more humbling for Jordin than seeing the impact he has on kids, both in his own community and in other Aboriginal communities across Canada.

Jordin also gives back to the community in other ways. But unlike many celebrities,

Jordin Tootoo is a role model for Aboriginal youth.

he does it quietly and with little fanfare. He has led hockey camps in Aboriginal communities, makes school visits to talk about the importance of education, and takes very seriously his status as a role model for young people.

"I'm the stepping stone for those kids," he says. "I'm paving the way." He travels the

Aboriginal Hockey Heroes

One of the players Jordin Tootoo admired growing up was former NHLer Theoren Fleury. Fleury is of Métis heritage. Fleury had to borrow an old pair of skates and a broken stick to play his first game at the age of five. Later, as a member of the Calgary Flames, Theo was four-time winner of the Molson Cup, given to distinguished players. But Tootoo also admired Fleury for his size. At just 168 centimetres (5 feet 6 inches), Fleury proved that height doesn't equal strength in the NHL.

country, breaking down barriers and showing Aboriginal kids what they can achieve.

All across Canada, there are kids playing shinny on lakes and rinks, just like Jordin and Terence used to do. Each one of them pretends to be a hockey star. Some of them dream of being number 22.

"It puts a smile on my face," Jordin says. "To be an inspiration is always uplifting. It's a small community and it's a huge honour that they look up to me." He remembers a time when he was one of those kids, pretending to be Wendel Clark or Theo Fleury and collecting hockey cards of his favourite players. Now kids collect his cards, own his bobble-head doll, and wear his jersey proudly.

One message he strives to pass on is the need for a good education. Jordin knows that he won't always be a hockey player. For him, finishing high school and getting his diploma was the first step to his future.

Off-Season Work

The first part of the off-season is spent recovering from injuries and resting. The rest of the summer is spent gradually building up fitness. Players spend time at NHL training camps. Their days and diets are planned and a fitness program is designed for each athlete. Players train twice a day, five days a week, and take two days off for recovery and regeneration.

"My parents had a rule of no school, no hockey. Hockey will always be there, but an education is the most important part of being successful in life." Jordin tells kids that with an education, the sky is the limit. With an education, doors will open.

According to Jordin, the hardest part of playing in the NHL is staying in the NHL. A player has 82 regular season games and, with any luck, 12 or more playoff games. A hockey player has to be in top physical condition and avoid injuries. During the off-season, all players, including Jordin, have to train just as hard to stay in shape and be ready for the next year.

Pro hockey players have a reputation for staying out late and partying hard. But an athlete who wants his career to progress has to be very careful about drinking alcohol and eating junk food. There are millions of dollars on the line and younger hockey players are waiting to take their spot. Most NHL players take their off-season as seriously as they take hockey season.

Even with all the training that he has to do, Jordin spends summers at home in Rankin Inlet. He never forgets where he came from or who he is. Back home he's not just a hockey star. People at home know him as the little guy who grew up there. "It's nice to get away from being an NHL player," he says. Far from the glare of

Jordin ice fishing at home in Rankin Inlet after reaching the NHL.

the spotlight, he can relax and be himself.

"Jordin is the dream son," a former mayor of Rankin Inlet once said. "He was like that before he became a superstar. If Jordin saw you with an extra bag of groceries, he would carry it for you."

Life is simple back home. People come and go through each other's homes as if they were their own. Everyone is welcomed as if they were family.

Jordin spends time with his family, hunting or sitting for hours in a boat with his father. Drifting in a large canoe on the calm waters of Hudson Bay, father and son talk easily. They laugh and banter like friends. They are in no hurry to get back home. It doesn't matter if they bring something home to Rose or not.

There are seals in the water, but they are difficult to hunt. With so little fat (or blubber) in the summer, the animals sink quickly. Jordin has been hunting with his father since he was six years old, but seal hunting is still a challenge for him. Barney and Jordin continue along Hudson Bay and see caribou grazing past the shore. The beluga whales will be migrating past

Rankin Inlet at the end of the summer.

These are the moments that will remain in Jordin's mind when he leaves to live out the dream again. It's the same dream that he and his brother trained their entire lives for. And every moment on the ice is a moment he can share with Terence, who isn't there but will never be far away.

He'll talk to his family every day when he's gone. But nothing replaces the everyday things he misses when he's back in Nashville with the Predators.

Jordin plays for himself, for his brother and family, and for all the kids who will come after him. He'll never forget who he is or where he comes from. But even with that pressure on him, when he steps out onto the ice and hears his name being chanted, he will just play. Play big. Play from the heart. He'll play the way he did when he was just a kid on the pond back home, checking the bigger kids into the boards at full speed. He'll draw his stick back for a killer slapshot that sounds like thunder. And he'll hear the words of his father in his head every time he steps onto the ice. "Fight your way through, Jordin." And that's exactly what Jordin Tootoo will do.

Glossary

Agitator: A player who annoys or distracts the other team by trash talking or starting fights.

Bantam league: Players in the Bantam league are under fifteen as of December 31 of the current season.

Charging penalty: A penalty given when a player jumps into the air before hitting another player or takes more than three strides before a hit.

ESPN: Short for Entertainment Sports Programming Network. ESPN is an American cable network that broadcasts sports programs.

Game misconduct penalty: A player given a game misconduct penalty is ejected immediately and sent to the locker room. If a player gets three in one season, he receives a one-match suspension.

Inuktitut: The Inuit language spoken in Nunavut.

Junior Hockey: A league for players aged twenty and under who are interested in playing college or professional hockey.

Linemates: The players who are on the ice in a line during the game. The forward line includes a left wing, a centre, and a right wing.

Linesmen: Officials who watch for violations involving the red or blue lines.

Molson Cup: A trophy presented monthly to the Canadian player who has the most three-star points, which are given by the media at the end of each game.

NHL Entry Draft: A yearly meeting of every NHL team where they select the rights to available players.

Roughing penalty: A penalty given when a player pushes or shoves an opposing player after the whistle has been blown.

Slapshot: The hardest shot in hockey.

Slashing: Swinging a stick at an opponent, whether contact is made or not.

Suspension: A punishment where the player is fined and not allowed to play for a number of games.

Western Hockey League: The highest level of Junior hockey based in western Canada and the Pacific Northwest. Part of the Canadian Hockey League.

World Juniors: The World Junior Hockey Championship is a yearly competition played by the top national teams from around the world.

Acknowledgements

First, a huge thank you to Jordin Tootoo for making time in his hectic schedule to speak to me. Thanks also to Kevin Wilson and Tim Darling of the Nashville Predators for answering questions and providing photos. Thanks to Ken Malenstyn and Big Red Barn Entertainment. Many of the quotes used in this book are from my own conversations with Jordin while others are from quotes he gave to the media throughout his career. Particularly helpful were the *Nunatsiaq News*, *USA Today*, *Sports Illustrated*, *ESPN The Magazine*, ESPN Online, CBC Sports, CBC News, *Hockey Digest*, and the *New York Times*.

About the Author

Melanie Florence is an Aboriginal writer based in Toronto. Her byline has appeared on everything from online dating advice for men to a piece about not so perfect parenting; from an interview with Meg Cabot to a review of an award-winning Aboriginal dance performance. She is also the author of the upcoming title *Canada Apologizes: Native Residential Schools*, published by Formac Publishing Company Ltd. Melanie is mom to Josh (6) and Taylor (4) who are still unimpressed with her career because she's not Robert Munsch.

Photo Credits

We gratefully acknowledge the following sources for permission to reproduce the images in this book:

Courtesy of Allan and Eunice Beaver: p 87

Courtesy of Jordin Tootoo: p 15, p 17, p 19, p 20, p 21, p 24, p 25, p 28, back cover (top) and p 33, p 35, p 47, p 56, p 92, cover (top).

Courtesy of the Nashville Predators: p 64, cover.

Courtesy of Tashia Smith: p 69, back cover (middle) and p 75, back cover (bottom) and p 81, p 83.

Index

More gripping underdog tales of sheer determination and talent!

⊙ RECORDBOOKS

Recordbooks are action-packed true stories of Canadian athletes who have changed the face of sport. Check out these titles available at bookstores or your local library, or order them online at www.lorimer.ca.

Big Train: The legendary ironman of sport, Lionel Conacher
  by Richard Brignall

China Clipper: Pro football's first Chinese-Canadian player, Normie Kwong by Richard Brignall

Crazy Canucks: The uphill battle of Canada's downhill ski team
  by Eric Zweig

Fearless: The story of George Chuvalo, Canada's greatest boxer
  by Richard Brignall

Fighting for Gold: The story of Canada's sledge hockey Paralympic gold
  by Lorna Schultz Nicholson

Jarome Iginla: How NHL's first black captain gives back by Nicole Mortillaro

Lacrosse Warrior: The life of Mohawk lacrosse champion Gaylord Powless
  by Wendy A. Lewis

Long Shot: How the Winnipeg Falcons won the first Olympic hockey gold
  by Eric Zweig

Pink Power: The first Women's World Hockey Champions
  by Lorna Schultz Nicholson

Small Town Glory: The story of the Kenora Thistles' remarkable quest for the Stanley Cup by John Danakas and Richard Brignall

Something to Prove: The story of hockey tough guy Bobby Clarke by Nicole Mortillaro

Star Power: The legend and lore of Cyclone Taylor
  by Eric Zweig

Tough Guys: Hockey rivals in times of war and disaster
  by Eric Zweig

Winning Gold: Canada's incredible 2002 Olympic victory in women's hockey by Lorna Schultz Nicholson